A Time for Winter

by Kait Quinn

Copyright © 2019 Kait Quinn

All rights reserved. No part of this book may be reproduced in any manner whatsoever without written permission of the author except in the case of reprints in the context of reviews.

"Either Way" was originally published in the Spring 2015 issue of *New Literati*.

Interior Artwork:
Rain cloud icon made by Eucalyp from flaticon.com
Leaf and Tree icons made by Freepik from flaticon.com
Sprout icon made by Nikita Golubev from flaticon.com

ISBN-13: 9781795286510

For the broken, the lonely,
the lost, the hurting,
the seekers of light,
belonging, and healing.
You are not alone.
The darkness is just part
of the journey.

CONTENTS

Hurt	1
Burn	51
Heal	67

HURT

Before I could shed
the dead weight,
I had to confront
the darkness.

Minor Chord Infection

Somewhere between cassette tapes,
compact discs,
illegally downloaded mp3s,
& wine-stained,
out-of-tune piano keys,
a minor chord slipped up beneath
my cherry-painted fingernails,
pulsed into my bloodstream,
& made itself a home
in my gummy little heart.

How to Explain It

If only for a moment
you could curl up
into my veins,

then maybe, you would understand
why my limbs sway back
& forth

between bending backwards
        & stagnancy.

Or why my vision blurs
& my eyes sink back in-
to their salt-crusted craters.

Or why my lips bleed,
bones jut out,
sweat glues my back to the mattress.

Or why my head feels like
a hurricane, & my heart
—my heart just lies there
: quiet eye of the storm.

When Flowers Bloom

> *April is the cruellest month, breeding*
> *Lilacs out of the dead land, mixing*
> *Memory and desire, stirring*
> *Dull roots with spring rain.*
> *Winter kept us warm, covering*
> *Earth in forgetful snow, feeding*
> *A little life with dried tubers.*

> *from "The Waste Land" by T.S. Eliot*

The sky falls in April
in big drops of break ups
& nostalgia,
bad news, infidelities, & goodbyes.

When the snow melts,
I remember how loud the world is—
birds, crickets, & lawn mowers,
my pulse breaking out into a sweat.

Trees die in November;
everything else dies in April:
marriages, friendships,
childhood, grandparents,

that girl with whom I'd briefly planned
to publish a sappy poetry book
but never did
because I blindly chose the boy
we were both foolishly sleeping with.

That boyfriend left me for someone else in April.
The next one left the country a year later.

At 16, my virginity
flapped off the bare back of a graduating senior
& landed, stringless, on his unvacuumed floor
to roll under his bed & die
among the dust bunnies, old car parts, & forgotten,
unlaundered clothes.

All I'm saying
is that flowers bloom at funerals.

My Madness is Not the Same as Yours

A madness stirs in each of us,
knocks against our rib cages and bowels,
sends our hearts aflutter, our tongues to curl
back into our throats.

My madness is not the same as yours.
It sits quietly in the heart of my belly
and wakes at the most opportune moment,
for it, not I.

It flings me into bed,
spews salt from my eyes,
sends an earthquake to rattle my bones,
shed me of my skin.

Your madness may drive you forward
or pull you back, rush adrenaline
through your veins
or make you hesitate.

My madness keeps me still
enough to relive everything I've done
and everything I haven't
over and over again.

Stuck

I can't explain
why I feel as if my shoulders
have dropped out of their sockets,
or why

nightly,
the hollow cavities in my abdomen
blossom   into one big void that
by morning, seems to define me.

And I can't put a finger on why
after three years of absence and violent sways of your heart,
you still cross my mind,

or why my pulse picks up speed
when that song comes on,
conjuring memories I thought I'd long forgotten.

I can't tell you why I spend my nights
awake—
tossing, turning, and aching

—or for what or whom
these eyelids get stuck open
re-watching everything that has and hasn't happened,

        as if it will change a thing.

Listen

If I etched you onto
my skin then,
you wouldn't know it
now.
        But brace yourself on
the sticky side of my ribs
& hear
        the rage of oceans
        tossed in a hurricane,
        the penetrating moan
        of rooted wood in winter,
        the wail of a heart string—
        how it pulls & snaps
—the guttural howl
of impending death.

Dead Weight

I've held this feeling before,
one as palpable as a stone
in the palm of my hand.

The weight of ten years ago
drags itself up and down my throat,
settles into my stomach lining,

dies somewhere deep in the bowels
until a picture, a damp, leaf-scented wind,
a minor chord progression

I've never heard until just now
reanimates the dead weight of you,
pulling me back instead of forward

        the same way you did then.

Either Way

I can't tell
if it's the morning chill

        or your name on my lips

that sends my skin
to shiver.

        (I can neither
        sip you up
        nor spit you out—

        you cling to me like fresh ink,

        hovering just above
        and beneath
        the surface.)

Either way,
winter is upon me.

Inhabitant

I attempt to sleep off
a hardness inside me,
and in the morning, it gives the illusion of dissipating,

only to grow back throughout the shifting day.
A solution: to sleep forever. This cannot be,
for if a lifetime is spent asleep, I might as well be dead.

I do not eat,
but I can only ignore the ravenous groans inside me
for so long—I feed, and I harden.

A tub topped with scented froth
seems a promising remedy.
From a room away, I listen to the rush of warm water—

the malignant mass climaxes in its growth,
expanding and willing
and ready to be extracted into the warmth.

Plath herself believed there was nothing
a warm bath could not cure.
This I have proven true on many occasions before:

To the twist of cramping and the anger of stomachs!
To the mental afflictions!—lost love, lost sleep, lost mind.
And to the cliché!—the resuscitation of dead romance.

Yet this would result in palish, damaged skin,
wrinkled and withered like a sun-dried grape.
From what:

old age or a longer than planned submergence?
Whichever comes first
before the hardness inhabited in me is excised.

So which is it: an uncomfortable fullness,
or is this the dead weight of emptiness?
There is a harshness in conflicting cures of an unknown sickness.

Mental Distress at Midnight

Nightly, my eyes bat open,
brain inflamed and whirring,
reaching out through the irises
so as not to crash and disperse
against the skull like ocean swells
against the side of a cliff.

1 a.m.—
my torso springs off the mattress,
arms cross my chest like the bones
are magnetic, hands grip my shoulders
to keep them in their sockets.
I stay like that, upright in bed,
holding my body together,
until I slow my breath and convince myself
that my bones are still intact.

I cocoon into a blanket to halt
all talks
between body and brain.
I count my breaths, wait for morning,
and try not to think about
what my body is trying to tell me.

Unraveled

I knew this day would come,
as sure as the unwinding
of a scarf from the neck,
the unraveling of thread
from a baby blanket—
thirty years ancient,
soft with security,
imprinted with teeth marks
holding on for dear life.
For years it sat in my belly,
collecting fear and anxiety,
feasting on confidence
and joy until all I had left
was withered: head down,
shoulders sloped, mouth
sagged, eyes averted.
Some days I'm so deflated,
I can't fathom the heart,
the blood, the organs
inside me, save the bones—
the bones I understand:
their strength and their fragility,
the way they grind together
or break apart.
How I really knew I'd lost it—
nerve endings frayed,
brain dark
—was when I thought my arm
had bent backwards
or my shoulder had fallen out
of its socket, and I couldn't tell
if it was real or if
it was all in my head.
And now I feel like I'm just
waiting
for the neck to collapse,
the last thread to unravel.

Nocturne

I.
Midnight: insomnia strikes.
Ghosts arise
where there are none,
and the cat roams
his castle, howling nocturnes.

II.
What I would give to be
unconfined by the circadian
rhythm, to navigate
the shadows, watch stars
bloom into dawn.

Turn

Eyelids grow heavy,
heartbeat drops slow
and steady; the skin,
once taut, now spreads
and settles like the sea over sand.
But the head doesn't follow
the dying body's command.
My eyes go hollow,
moonlight painting
my skin vampirical
—no heat radiates
from my torso and limbs,
no fresh blood
circulates the veins.
The heart has stopped
and gone cold,
churning my blood to ice.
Only in daylight
do I find rest: O, how the sun
sets my skin afire,
brings my pupils to pulsate
to a piercing ache!
I succumb to dawn
and the hurt in my eyes—
their lids like night,
the bed an open grave
—until dusk sets
and I rise from the dead,
sharp-toothed and hungry
for a living,
pulsing
vein.

Death Thoughts

awake
& unable

to cool my skin
& still my bones,

to silence
images

        of oblivion

reeling through
my head.

The Storm

The driving rain came down on the roof
like sticks and stones,
like sharp sheets of nails,
like a stampede of wildebeest hooves
trampling anything underfoot
down into the dirt.
My lungs gasped for air
as if they were drowning.
Even the noon day sun, beaming down
from a cloudless sky, could feel like a storm,
a heaving hurricane beating against my chest
with closed, raging fists.
No—some days not even sunlight,
with her cinnamon-spiced limbs,
could prick & prod & drag me out of bed.
Once I was brave enough to peer over the edge
only to find a rising sea,
waves peaking & falling & swirling:
little gaping mouths gulping
down socks & salt I tossed off the bed,
hungry for bone & flesh.
So I receded
back into my makeshift womb,
warm & soft & dark & safe,
curling up to wait out the storm
—the rain that falls like stones,
like nails,
the rain that falls like spooked wild hooves,
the rain that falls
& never stops.

Beneath The Current

A shadow washes over me like the sea
washing over the shore,
only shadows don't ebb back
as quickly as they flowed.

I turn away from the sun streaming
in from the window—its rays are fingers
wrapped in flames on my cold, sallow skin.

I watch the sunlight dance where the wall
meets the roof, but it moves
        s l o w   like the sun is drowsy,
like it's under the ocean, buoyed
by salt, my eyelids caked with it.

My limbs lie weighted under water,
my lungs fill with the sandy brackishness of it.
I can't recall the moment
I lost track of direction—floor is ceiling,
ceiling is wall is ceiling is floor.

Every now and then, my eyes
meet a window, and I glean just enough
strength to bang on the burning glass,
scream at the top of my lungs, but
no sound comes out, no words form,
my lungs as empty
as my head,
bobbing continuously into the walls.

Lonely

Am I supposed to tell you
how bad it gets?
That I feel loneliness the way you'd feel a bullet
lodge into your chest?

I feel like these are the feelings
we're supposed to keep hushed.
These are the feelings we're not
supposed to feel because
it could be worse,
it could be a bullet,
and we're supposed to feel grateful
for what we have.

I have everything,
and I have nothing.

And honestly,
I don't think I can keep carrying the weight of it,
the stomach-empty weight
of loneliness.

The feeling of unlocking the front door
as quick as you can
because any second,
all your insides will come spilling out.

The feeling of wishing you'd never come home at all,
its emptiness piercing.

The feeling that makes you curl up small
& cry, cry, cry
until you're floating somewhere
on a bed of salt
between life and death.

Somewhere numb, somewhere safe,
somewhere far from yourself,
where the heart and the brain and the blood
can't get to you.

Are these things that I'm supposed to tell you?
Because some days I don't think
I can bottle it up,
no matter how much I want to.

Still

I'm trying (trying
trying
trying)
to hold myself
together, to not
waste away
          into nothing.

But my arms are bent backwards
& pulled from their sockets,
my thighs disconnect from the hips,
my tongue swells to a sticky slug,
my head is a pool of blood
threatening to roll off
my crooked little neck,
& it terrifies me
          into absolute stillness.

The Heart

The heart can only take
so much.
When it's had
quite enough,
the heart gives up
—my heart stops.

Rain

The rain started and didn't stop
for three days. Some rains fall
for a five-year stretch. Some rains
aren't made of recycled water
and flecks of sky. Some rains
are knives, slicing through flesh,
bone, down into the heart.
Some rains are floods
that make dead weight of bodies.
My body is a log,
lodged in a muddy river bed.

Passive

Nothing bleeds,
nothing hurts.
There's only numb
gnawing at my innards
—head full of static,
heart hollowed out.
I don't know what to love
or hate or want
anymore.
I just need to feel
foreign skin on mine,
& I don't know how
to explain that
to a sane mind.
Past lives don't rise
up from the dead,
the future can't get a rise
out of me,
& I'm too chaotic
to stay present.
I am a hostage
waiting
for something to happen
or for it all to end.

Should Be Poet

I had all day to be nothing but a poet.
I could have given you two poems, one haiku,
a lung, and a leg.

But I didn't feel like splitting open today,
spilling my salt and blood onto paper
and rearranging it
into strands of pearls and shiny things on strings.

They say writers should write every day,
but when you only know how to write from the soul,
writing every day takes its toll
on sutured and re-sutured hearts
and burnt-out brains.

So I would have given you a better poem
than this last-minute effort
patched together with glue and string,
but only saliva rolled across my tongue,
only blood ran through my veins.

Hollow

Life—or a lack of
—has left me completely
hollowed out.

Imposter

Is it fair to call myself a poet
if all
I do
is lie blank,
letting words I greedily devour
wither, rot, and decay?

What Am I

What
am
I
but a shell: a pale,
fragile little thing
with pretty blue marbles
planted in my skull
to distract the other bags
of meat and bones
from the emptiness
raging
behind them?

Stale

This body is a cave—
listen to the bones:
their rattles echo out
from the nose.

The eyes, when they dilate,
are a black expanse
of nothing: a sky without stars,
the Mariana Trench.

No spark ignites your flesh
when it comes into contact
with mine—no heat left,
no electricity.

I'm as hollow as a drum,
a bag of bones wrapped in flesh,
an empty shell, a bad cliché.
Bang against my chest,

hear it for yourself
(if you must), then be gone
before my emptiness crawls
into you from off my tongue.

Domesticated

Curled up
on the bed:
fetal,
cat-like.
Palms gripping
feet as if
to keep
from running
off.
Each brief escape
out
the back door
a bittersweet
taste
of what
came before.

Inhuman

Slowly, silently
the moon drops,
casting shiny pebbles across
Earth's eyes,
an eerie glow
on its shadows.

I thought that light was supposed to extinguish
the dark,
pull it up by the roots,
        not feed on it

—or is that my tooth,
sinking steadily into my arm?

O, how I wish I could pull my monstrous heart
up by its roots,
slowly, silently
skid it like a luminescent
pebble across a pond.

Maybe then
my flesh would stop bleeding,
and your golden limbs, of which
I am undeserving,
could tangle free from me
and firmly, rhythmically root into a heart
more human
than mine.

Disfiguration

I fall asleep with mirrors, searching
for perfection,

but the strangers,
stepping into my light,
wear costumes and masks
grown out of their skin;
their eyes all pupil—
I see my reflection in them.

If I sit under this heat
long enough,
would I, too, melt in the sun
and sprout wings on my back
or tentacles in my hair;
would the sweat on my brow
        leak
          into a tiger's face
                around my eyes:

the only hint of myself
under the disfiguration?

Starved and distorted,
they devour me—

can't they taste the remains of Narcissus
on their tongues,
        or are mirrors deceiving?

I look into my vanity,
breathe through the gills on my neck, touch
the black stripes tattooed to my skin—
the claws beneath my knuckles
a surprise
        that leaves a streak
                of dripping red   across my cheek.

Will anyone who knew me before

recognize the ocean—still alive
and swirling—
under the disfigurement?

I've stood before mirrors
for far too long.
Now I sit
in rooms too dark for reflections,   hiding
my hideous new form.

The mirror mocks my latest disfigurement—
       I have no sword to slay it,
        no flower to bear my name.

I fall asleep with mirrors, obsessed
with the stranger looking back,

for even I, in the luster of windows,
the surface of puddles,
the glass of pupils,
cannot see the churn
of blue and grey: the only hint
of myself
beneath the disfiguration.

Ghost Hour

Lying there
on the cheap blue
faux vintage rug,
blotches of tree-shaped shadows
turning dawn's sky
into a bruise,
my existence known only to the cat
sprawled beside me—
his spiked tongue scraping
against my eyelid, doting on me
like I was newborn
or wounded,
was my only solace
in those quiet morning hours,
(inky, then bleeding,
then glaucous)
when I am more ghost
than flesh.

Loneliness

Today I learned loneliness
oozes out from the body
as blood
as tears
as sighs
as a spasmic cry blooming from guttural ache.

Ultimatum

That old emptiness that lives deep
within me—under the skin,
inside the bones,
meandering down the intestinal halls—
is louder now than ever.

I've known
since I was sixteen
that my body is all I have
and a body isn't enough.

But I'm too old now to fill the gaps
with vodka & wolves,
childish games & fairy tales.

I just want to be someone
or nothing at all.

The Lost Poet

So I find myself (again)
latching onto every poem
my peers have ever written,
as if each line dripped
with honey, as if I could
swallow them down,
hatch a little poet
inside me: a poet with a brain
like a dictionary
or a library, a poet with
a rolling tongue,
skin like a sponge,
heart like a flower
fully bloomed, shedding pollen
onto every set of limbs
that mean to land
on my skin, unravel me,
and leave behind their dust
made up of everyone
they've ever been.

Instead, I jerk back
at touch, too afraid
of attachment, too afraid
to lose another
piece of my patchy innards,
scraped out
like a carved pumpkin
by people who didn't
deserve them. If only
I'd known then that each
loss is a gain, that my gut
breeds intuition. Maybe I,
too, could write poems
on politics, religion,
a wild woman's ways,
clipped down to the essentials,
rich with nuance and experience.

Instead I spend a whole hour
writing surface-level ditties

bloated with filler words and regret.
Instead I spend forty percent
of my energy
trying not to cry
at work, during a movie,
in front of my therapist.
Instead I eat lunch at my desk
in an office with walls
that don't touch the ceiling
so that I can hear
how easy it is
for everyone else.
Instead I hide in corners,
behind headphones and book spines
avoiding eye contact like pupils
will turn me into stone.
Instead I wear a mask so thick
I don't even recognize
myself.

What insight did I bring
to the table? For what
did I waste a whole hour?

Water Weight

I wanted to swim across the sea of my insecurity,
let the waves of fear & shyness pummel me deep
down into the darkest caverns of my fluid, salty soul
until I broke through the surface, lungs gasping
for air, fingers grasping skin, your palm
clasping to mine: two halves of a clam
sealing off its fragile innards from beaked
& tooth-nailed predators, clinging together
when currents pluck
& pull them from sand beds, escaping the binding
& splitting of nets, all the while working
a parasite into a pearl: an iridescent parapet
for which greedy hands would break apart
hundreds of clams to steal.

But I let the weight of it fill
my throat & drag me back to shore
where I watched you dive head first
into waves, out from jaws,
live, mate, two halves becoming whole,
molding pain into pearls,
while I shriveled in the sun, rubbed salt from my eyes,
limbs buried deep in the sand.

Written in the Stars

I can't resist it—
the darkness,
the salt soaked walls.
It doesn't make sense
that my mind calms
when I give
to pitch black,
fetal curve of shells.
And it does.
I can't help that I was born
clawed & hard-backed,
ice cracking through my irises,
heart exposed,
a perpetual roar stuck in my throat.

A Fate Like Loo Bella

Who left Loo Bella in the wych elm
—body warm and stuffed in a trunk
uncut from the ground?
Its great roots reach out
to grasp her hand, cut off and buried
nearby in the dirt—animal hoarding?
a witch's ritual? unfinished business
of the dead?

Townsfolk attempt to piece back together
the woman in a mustard skirt
and striped sweater
whose skull was not a bird's egg,
whose teeth were unmistakably crooked,
whose body, the doctor said,
had not gone cold
before someone encased it in a casket
still rooted to the earth,
whose pelvic bone revealed a mother,
whose identity was mistaken for another,
whose nameless remains
and undisturbed burial ground
showed signs of someone forgotten.

What details will they remake me from
when they find me inevitably forgotten?
Cracked forehead, barren hips,
teeth that never wore braces,
a tuft of copper still clinging to my skull
like marcescent leaves in winter,
skeletal fingers clutching a fork or pencil
or an old iPod that probably died
during Lana's crooning or something autumnal,
bones exposed,
half-draped in laundry-day clothes
and disintegrating into the dust
collecting on old books—
none bearing my name
—and surfaces void
of anything
but more dust.

Distortion

She lies beneath the deep sea's murk: honeyed voice,
barnacled limbs,
kelp hair blossoming from her scalp
like a maned lioness.

Her enigmatic songs, as warm
and sweet
as summer's setting suns,
fall as banshee screams upon dry ear drums.

If her eyes are the ocean's sapphiracal expanse,
her heart is its unrest—

>
> she'd give up her soul to shed
> her calcified scales for bare skin,
> her mellifluous voice for breath.

Minnehaha Falls, September 2017

As I watched the water surge in little currents
downstream, I wanted to wonder how fast
the creek was flowing, what causes it to rush past,
then churn, every so often, foaming at the mouth,
what it sounds like to stand in the space between
the rock slab and the falls, whether they freeze in winter.

But all I could wonder was how much
it would hurt to feel hundreds of tons
of water barrel down on my head,
how hard the baby rapids could slam my ribs
against the rocks, smooth with erosion, slick
with algae, how quick water fills the lungs.

And in some moments, there was nothing
to think about, only a quiet communion with
the wafting mist, leaves the maple trees dropped
down beside me, the silent shift from summer to fall
hovering in the air, the water moving
forward without fear or attachment or thought.

Still, with all of nature's reminders wrapped
around me and shoved under my nose, I couldn't fathom
stepping one foot in front of the other
nor stillness. I couldn't imagine a downstream,
a new season, what it would feel like
to let the dead weight of three decades drop.

Ghost

I have fought tooth and nail
for pain, comfort,
predictability,
and enslavement to ego.
But I've never fought for my own life.

What does it mean—
when death passes through you like a ghost?

Scars

You asked me about the scars on my arm.
I sucked in my breath and told you
they were from the cat,

like I told the girls in my freshman gym class
when I was fifteen and the wounds were fresh.
They didn't believe me either.

I am malaise in human form,
so I understand why you might think these
tiny, re-fleshed strings holding me together

were self-inflicted and these accumulating bruises
are from knocking into fists instead of coffee table edges,
crashing into elbows instead of doors.

Sometimes there is no epic to bandage a scar,
no battle for wounds, no tragedy
to explain the needles that held joints together
and the holes they left behind
after the bones grew back.

Guilt

Where are my atrocities?
What will send me back reeling
off so high a cliff
that I grab onto life
with a white-knuckled grip,
sweat and sob my way
to solid earth,
emptied of fears
I left splattered
across the jagged floor
of rock bottom?
Instead,
my body just
b l o a t s with guilt.

Drift

I found myself in the ocean—

salt buoyed me up to the surface
sending supper-plucking birds
fluttering up

        into the clouds.

Their feathers were white,
but the sunset turned them

        into silhouettes.

Their wings cast shadows over me
like a sheet pulled over a corpse.

I floated along for days,
wondering:

        where do I sail
        from here?

Worth of Pain

What is all this pain   worth?
What blooms
           when salt soaked?

       If the heart is a muscle,
will it self repair
              unraveled strings
              and microscopic tears,
rips at the seams
that left me gaping,
exposed to rust and rot?

       What do I feed the heart
to make it heal,
for who would curl up
in this decay;

              what could grow
              from this dark place?

BURN

Before I could heal,
I had to burn.

Scented

Some days I smell like rose petals & lavender.
Some days I waft into rooms like the skunk-stench of weed.
I shed cocoa & vanilla, sweat salt & strawberry.
Mostly I think I'm akin to fresh rain
seeping into fall's damp, dying leaves.

Youth

The days of youth
fall behind us,
along with the pines, gold foliage,
and winter dust.

Along with the sprawl
of forest trails, frog-rippled creeks,
the cold slap of a swimming pool
against ripe skin in January.

Along with the purple blossoms
on my lips and between my thighs.
Along with costumes, vodka,
poetry books, and stained glass eyes.

I never thought much of youth
until now
as I step across the threshold
into the vast unknown,

and I can't keep from clinging on
to what is dying.
So goes the clock,
so I try to carry on,

so goes the drag of my skin,
the slope of my shoulders,
the dead weight of youth on my back.

Summer Blues

I want to feel the crunch
of dried grass beneath my feet,
snag of leaves
tangled in my hair,

sunlight & snap
of crisp noon air,
cool & warm against
my skin   all at once.

I want to smell the dance of sage
& juniper, apple & balsam,
bathe in October's falling jewels
—pomegranate red, citrine gold.

O, to be simultaneously
living & dying   all at once,
autumn's harmony
plucking flesh from bone.

But all I feel is the dead weight of my skin
clinging to the bed linens,
the tug of sleep pulling
down my eyelids: swallowed up
          by mid-summer smog.

The Arrangement

Alone, not lonely,
I noticed the table there.
We were the same,
the arrangement and I:

off in a corner and vacant.
I only sat nearby
because I understand the lack
of wanting company.

Dead leaves were littered
around its legs.

He told me once
that I smell like autumn leaves.
He knows I like the fall.

Sitting apart in our arrangement,
guarded by the scent of November,
we connect,
in a way only we understand.

Burden

I wonder what it is—
the sorbet colors of sunsets,
dawn's warm cheek on her surface,
her vastness rocking eternally
from tranquility to turbulence

—that brings the ocean to tears
constantly;
her eyelids, briefly
filling with water and salt,
rubbed raw with the things

she can no longer carry:
a tangle of seaweed,
a dead jellyfish,
bottles of heartache and soul-stuff she was
unwillingly burdened with.

The Heart Has Not Stopped

What would it take
to set the heart going:
a melody
a touch
a shift between seasons,
an electric shockwave
between metal & flesh?

For years,
my heart has lied stagnant,
and I don't know how
much longer I can go on
without that familiar stir
behind my caged bones
when the heart's working
at full speed,
when summer slips silently
into fall,
when piano keys dance
with violin strings
& poems glide
across tongue
like honey,
when your fingertips hover
just out of reach
of my electric, levitating skin.

It is far past time
for the numb season
to end,
to shed
my dead skin,
expose raw nerve
& f e e l
everything
all at once
like I was carved
from salt & star
to do.

Cornucopia

Fall fell in the way only fall
does: cold drifts pull
sun rays and stardust
down through the trees in a slow drag.

My feet parade through Earth's confetti,
by November, crunched down to ash:
we've won something; we've lost something, too.
But O! This bounty! This dying makes us grateful!

Our knees are stained with it;
our skin pricks up at its call!
Each gust of wind is nostalgia, each leaf a jewel—
O, of all the seasons, the liveliest is fall!

Swell & Release

Clouds swelled in the sky overnight while we vacationed in our heads, oblivious to weather patterns in our preoccupation with drownings, ice queens, and Southern Baptist renditions of Shakespeare plays.

By mid-morning, the sky cracked open, releasing electricity, water weight, the mounting tension of thick, moist summer heat.

Running in humidity is akin to letting go. Every outside event, self judgement, and negative thought is a bead of salt and water pulsing out of pores, rolling off skin, colliding and dispersing against asphalt and cement. Every morning, people release themselves to dirt trails, concrete, and coastlines.

The earth is built on our dead weight.

Natural

I released myself back to the earth that birthed me
from between its blood-soaked thighs:
a fluid sac of mud & flesh carved from bone,
seed, & earth-
worm excrement.
I felt at home under the bellies of snails & toads,
peering into the slit pupils of snakes,
the spiders spindling their evening webs,
dew-dropped & moonlit,
waiting to decay with the leaves of summers past.

Cusp

How beautiful it is
to see things
living & dying
all at once
—the soft sway
of bare branches,
how the scarlet leaves dance
& descend,
crunch down to mosaics
beneath my feet,
a cold snap inhaling
summer's
last
breath.

Lean In, Let Go

There was little to be said
once the moon grew full
and the leaves dropped dead,
only to lean in to autumn's pull
and the decay inside my head.

Once old blood and new had brewed to a peak,
we scraped our peace from our tongues,
then sat silent beneath the leaves
until I was ready to the let the dead tumble off
the way Mother season taught me.

There is little left to say
now that the trees are bare
and the sky's gone grey,
only to stand weightless, palms up in the air,
naked limbs dancing beneath the sun's golden rays.

How to Heal

Hearts break like fever
breaks into a sweat,
like muscles rip
under tension
& sun peels off of flesh.

Like the Phoenix can't rise
out of ash without burning,
nor Earth bloom
without shedding dead weight,
breaking
is the first step
toward healing;
feeling it is the second.

November

Quieting,
rooting down,
taking it in:
the dark,
the light,
the parts of me that have died
& fled off
with October's final burn,
the lingering wisps of smoke
that
will
r i s e
in a slow sleep
to make room
for the parts of me
waiting
to bloom.

HEAL

Before I could blossom,
I had to still
quietly among the ashes
of the woman I thought
I was
& the woman I am
to become.

Reality

I wake to what I think
is a soft spring rain,
but a harsh glint of sunlight
confronts my pupil,
and the rain is snow melting.
Afternoon naps are so disorienting,
I think to myself.
But when I fell asleep,
the world was dark and star deep.
I roll over, refusing
to face the bright beams of reality,
its melting and shedding light,
its limbs and buds that blossom
while I stay rooted to winter,
sticking to sheets like snow sticks
to shadows and tongues to ice.

A Time for Winter

Say it: say that I am dead,
and I'll root my feet
into the earth,
unfold my lips: into petals: into your palms,
shed summer from my shoulders.

There is a time for winter,
for mending the bones, freezing off
the dead things
so new life can grow
more lush, more violet.

The slabs of ice caked over my irises
will melt into lakes,
these lips one day will bloom.
But summer has lasted a decade:
I am in the winter of my youth.

Feeling It

As I looked inward—in the guts of my chest
and the folds of my bowels—
I found blue velvet oceans,
streams of black silk. Violet waves of blood
and salt, atoms and starstuff
crashed over me, painting me plum
and crimson
as they dragged away and back
to those dark and sticky parts of me—
thick, messy, coated with dust.
        I draw back
—I draw back and gasp for breath,
coaxing my lungs to breathe deeper
and deeper and deep enough to wade through
the deepest crevices and thickest muck
of my witchy, wolf-woman soul.

Solar

from just the right distance
my eyes / are solar systems
equipped with little planets / moons
caked in ice & filmed
with stardust / my eyes
: windows
to another galaxy / tell me
of their gravity

Sun Salutations

Every morning I
s t r e t c h
my arms up
high, as if
to pull sun
from sky,
implant it
in my belly
hoping
its heat
will fuel me
into being.
Some days
the sun slips
right into
my fingers,
warming body
electric.
Some days
there are just
too many
clouds
to dig through,
slowing body
static.

Caught Off Guard

I.
Curious
how a hot sun
& crystal blue sky
can so suddenly
be swallowed
by thick veils of night.

II.
I am a lone wolf,
in the heart of winter,
without a tongue to lick my wounds,
without a pack to call me home.

Mute

Words tap on my throat,
gnaw at my tongue,
inching their way from heart to mouth.
But I gag them down
like horse pills
dry-swallowed down the esophagus.

I'm still learning to trust my gut,
open my heart,
access my intuition.
I'm still learning
to find my voice,
speak my truth,
let words tumble
out from my lips
like honey,
like sunlight,
like summer daisies
in bloom.

But my body remembers little violences
that keep me still;
my tongue suffers old wounds
that keep me mute.

Sometimes I Think the Poet in Me is Dead

        Sometimes I think the poet in me is dead.

Words that once bloomed
from my ventricles & veins—

at the drop of a tear, the change of seasons,
the moth-wing fluttering
of consecutively skipped heartbeats

—are now as dry as leaves in November,
shriveled up like an old lover's bouquet,
brown & grey, hanging from the ceiling.

Winter has curled up inside me,
stilled my heart & filled me up
with ice,

        a snowfall
        kind of quiet.

In the hollow silence, I wonder: if
the poet inside me has died,
then have I?

Strange Land

Sometimes I feel so disconnected from myself
—a stranger in my own skin.
I do the things I'm supposed to do
to go inward, circle back, feel, reconnect:
I yoga, I journal,
I sit or walk quietly, unplugged, with nothing
but the self.

But some days the self is so foreign & distant,
I stay plugged in, 24/7, to podcasts or TV,
completely bypassing music,
the one thing that ever made me feel like me.

I know that I'm completely lost
when I can't imagine what song I want to hear
& when all my favorite fallbacks inspire nothing but a nostalgia
so intense & sad & deep,
I can't bear to sit with it,
to feel the pain I need to feel
to make my skin a home again.

What Complexity:

to be both
living
& dying.
Every day I slip in
to new skin.
Every year I sag
& sink
a cell's worth more.
Shifts so small,
no one can see it
—but the body knows.
Is that age
or depression?
Is my body dying
or just my heart?
Is my heart dying
or just my soul?
My soul died already
when I was 14 years old,
when the reality of life
my adults
failed to teach me
sucked it right out
of my tiny child-like body.
I was not taught
to think,
to question,
to be curious.
I was taught to accept
what I was told.
Now I don't know who
or what
or how to love.
Now I am both
living
& dying,
too unsure to choose a side,
too apathetic
to go all in.

Purpose

I want nothing,
and I want everything.
Why is this all I've learned from living?

Where is my curiosity for life,
thirst for art, hunger for learning,
drive to act on compassion & empathy?
What is my purpose for being?

All I have is a soul yearning
to exist, to see
& be seen,
a pendulum heart
in endless swing.

Winter Comeback

glacial winds cocooned the house
in quiet howls
& cold snaps.

snow
fell,
first in flurries,
then in drifts

that buried raw
spring sprouts
beneath january ice.

—winter's last gasp.

Insomniac

All the ghosts and regrets that lingered in my head,
all the springs and summers I wished I was dead
come rushing, like a salty flood, back into my heartspace,
sending to writhe and wail
the atoms between bone & skin & skin & bed.

What so disturbs my heart when body-limp and eyes shut?
What leads me, alarmed and upright, to ghost-walk
about the house as if I am capable of haunting?
How many mornings can I wake sore-limbed and sallow-eyed
as if I've never slept a wink?

Visceral

It's not until
I sit down to write a poem
bubbling up inside me
that I realize
how in tune with my emotions
I used to be,
how out of touch
I am with them now.

It's not that I've pent them up
& buried them deep
in gaps between organs,
muscle, & bones.
It's that I forgot
how to feel,
how to lay my sensitivity bear
to every pierce, pleasure, tingle, & wrench,
how to turn
inside out
& go raw.

I used to feel you in my toes.
I used to feel him
in the unstitching of my heart seams.
I used to feel love, autumn, & music
circulate through my veins
like electricity.
I used to feel life, my lack of a place in it
like stones in my throat.
I felt loneliness
like a hurricane
tearing at my chest
until I felt completely
hollowed out.
Depression once felt like teeth
gnawing
at my nerve endings.

Now I'm lucky
if I feel anything at all.
But poetry

is slowly reteaching me
that everything
is visceral.

Edge of Winter

The frost on the leaves of dead flowers,
stilling spring from blooming and weeds
from their sprawl, was thick as icing
on a cake.

The morning fog was thicker,
seeping in through the nostrils,
settling deep in the lungs like
tar from a cigarette.

The cold can trick you into thinking
you're made of ice: each breath
comes in like a dagger,
out like winter fog.

Somewhere Between Sleep and Wake

I shut my eyes and wake up
on the other side of my eyelids
into Paris, into a car nose-diving
off a bridge, into the underground:
blue-tinged, arctic, caked with ice.

Every surface shakes as my partner
violently tosses against the mattress,
as I dodge crumbling dirt and rocks,
arms tossed over my head
like a helmet.

I ride the elevator down to level nine.
The cat's meowing fades to a muffle
the further I sink underground
until I can only hear water
drip and crack as it freezes to ice.
I emerge from the elevator, shivering,
my body working without me to cocoon the blankets.

Someone stirs in the distance,
something brushes against my leg.
A piercing cackle, or the cat's meow,
echoes through the gelid chambers.
A queen of ice rounds the corner
and looks me in the eye,
knowing more than I do, knowing what
lives down here, what grabs and bites.

Something cold presses up against my thigh,
and the cat's meowing has hollowed to a moan.
I look down, slowly registering the frozen corpse
gripping my ankle with its icicle fingers,
but my body is molasses. Its teeth pierce my flesh,
and I cry out in pain or let out a whimper.

Now that it's too late, my legs are like lightning.
I run to the elevator, manically pressing the button
that closes the door as the corpse lets out
a guttural guffaw, knowing more than I do
as the cat draws blood and the elevator stops.

Stuck between floors, I collapse in defeat:
an eternity underground, another corpse
for the ice queen.
But as my head hits the ground, my eyes flutter open,
lungs sucking in air like their fresh
from the womb, eyes adjusting, body tossing beside me,
the cat's meows filling up the bedroom.

Narcissus vs The Crow

Balancing on my toes,
knees splayed like a frog's,
I listen to the voice that says:
look into the pond;
what do you see?
I see,
or I try to. I try to
see rainbowed koi, shimmering,
instead of my dry, pale skin,
lackluster &
vitamin D-deficient.
I try to see seaweed swaying
in underwater rhythm
instead of my hair, tangled,
sparse, & limp.
I try
to catch a glint of sunlight
beaming off an oyster's pearl
instead of my dead eyes,
grey as winter, cold as ice.
But my arms can't carry
my weight, my toes can't detach
from the ground.
The pond is only my reflection—
today Narcissus has won.

Control

I can't help falling back
—certain scents, songs, & colors
from last year & yesterday & almost
a decade ago
push all the right buttons
to send me reeling
back to crisp weather
& collegiate simplicity,
to when I was chaotic,
self-destructive,
& alive,
to when everything,
even I,
fell
into place.

I know we're supposed
to move forward,
but my head is a time machine
(& my heart adores it)
& I'm still learning how
to control it
or deciding if I even want to.

The Heart Doesn't Know What It Wants

The heart doesn't know
what it wants. It latches
on, with its sticky strings,
to anything that knocks
against its doors,
rips the soul from
wandering eyes peering
through its open blinds.

The heart never ripens,
only buds and blossoms,
palms up and open,
devouring the world
wide-eyed, knocking against
the ribs, holding tight
to what it loves
with a small, sticky grip.

The heart knows
how to live, how to die,
how to go on when it's
cut out and fondled by
bare hands and placed back
into its chamber—sutured,
scarred, finger-
printed, and misshapen.

But the heart doesn't know why
it blooms, then breaks, then
blooms again, why it slows
and quickens, feels a tug
on every chord from every
direction, how it stretches wide
and snaps back without breaking.
The heart doesn't know what it wants.

Towerest of Towers

Having ascended the dark bowels
of the Cesky Krumlov Castle,
I stand at the top of the "towerest of towers,"
Renaissance-styled and tiered like a pastry,
proudly protruding from a small Czech town
plucked straight out of a fairy tale featuring
enchanted roses, beauty, and beasts.
I take the three sixty-degree route
'round the open-air peak, retracing century-
old steps once walked by guardsmen
and a mourning Rosenberg lady.
I stop long enough to feel the fresh spring air
frolick against my face,
to photograph the orange rooftops
surrounding the castle's crown—pasteled
like a cake and rivaled only by St. Jost's
turquoise cupola—and watch
the village sprawl into pastures, into hills
and stretch on to the horizon.
Suddenly,
I'm an ocean-tinged brogue
in the thick of the Atlantic, and I can't decide
if the wind's picked up or if all the breath
has escaped from my lungs,
as if for years, I hadn't been breathing.
Other tourists are waiting, cameras poised,
pupil behind lense, so I reluctantly descend
one hundred and sixty-two steps,
but I haven't stopped spiraling.

Quarter Life Crisis

My heart is as restless
as the sea,
my thoughts
intertwining like
tangled branches,
fragile & flighty
as dying leaves.
My lungs
purge howls
hollow
as a wolf's,
guttural
as a hungry cat's.
My eyeballs
can't stop taking
everything in.
When will the sun
meet my skin?
What shore
will I call home?

Curiosity

To ask
to learn
to know
is to enlighten
is to grow
is to take away
the magic
of not knowing.

— I know nothing.

On the Cusp

Through winter windows sheeted
with frost, a slice of green dances
on a naked branch—leaves pumping
like newborn Monarch wings.

Birds shake winter off in flurries;
their chirps slow-crawl
through window cracks like blood
crawls down a waking limb.

Someone paints the pine needles
green overnight while pink blooms
like petals from my cold blue lips
curtaining the windows in ice.

Ash

I haven't died in quite
some time. Sometimes I miss
the ashes,
smell of cedar in winter.

Sometimes
I hope they stay scattered
sans flowers
or flesh sprouting
from them—
only flames,
then dust.

And sometimes I will my skin
to stay sewn shut,
limbs intact,
red hair unplucked

because dying
isn't easy.
Coming back takes everything
out of me
—hear me hollow
out & empty.

All I want to shed from my skin
is you & yesterday & tomorrow.

All I want is to swell
with blood, water,
& heartbeats.

All I want is now
wrapped in namastes,
glowing skin,
& poetry.

Dive In

I hear
ocean waves
in the rise
and fall
of my
wintered
lungs,
feel tropics
bead along
my curves.

My hair is
strips of sunset
on the water's
lapping surface,
my skin
a stretch
of sand:
white,
freckled,
rippled with
flaws.

And my eyes—
my eyes
are glaucous
lagoons,
unpolished
jewels, blue bells,
contused flesh
with interminable
depths
beckoning
you
to dive in.

Will

>   *after "Elm" by Sylvia Plath*

I know the bottom. I know it with every
tooth, bone, and organ.
The bottom is a pit, thick
with swarms of earthworms squirming
in damp dirt.

I do not fear it. Death does not scare me
into living. Death cradles and rocks me
to sleep like I am a newborn baby,
only knowing the encasement of a womb,
the muffle of vocal chords,
the distant chime of fork against plate.

This echo behind my rib cage,
this gurgle in my belly: these
are my dissatisfactions.
I am nothing but empty.
I lie with my hands draped over
my breasts like I am ready.
I would cry, but I've stopped that.
I feel nothing but empty.

But some days I feel sunsets
burn into my skin until I glisten,
peached, full-bodied. Periodically,
the moon reminds me
my womanhood, dragging me out from the inside
until I feel the stains of life
seep out of me,
thighs sticky with it.

In these thin rips between storm clouds
dispersed, I unfurl myself from the grip of this
dark thing inside me and watch it flap out,
my skin in its mouth, looking for something else
to latch onto and kill.

I look to the same woman who taught me the art
of dying

for will.
I lean into Sylvia's rhythmic chant,
body full of blood, irony clenched
in my sweaty fist, and listen
to the cry of my heart,
the pulse in my wrist:
I am, I am, I am.

Inner Wild

I want to be in the forest
beneath comets and constellations,
jeweled canopies
that color my skin the way stained glass
paints an empty church—   its benches
still virtuous, its water holy.

I want to stand at the base
of a mountain,   look up
and feel small,
insignificant
before I crawl back
into my tent.
Come morning, I emerge
bent at the knees,
shoot my arms straight up
from the soles of my feet,
and greet her majesty
as an equal.

I want to feel the rush
of a creek, let the inner child
run wild as I hop
from mud to trunk to rock: Watch out
for sharks! Careful: hot lava!
Don't wake the dead!
—and what other perils awaited me
if I couldn't keep my balance.

Why wasn't I born
on the forest floor,
leaves between my toes,
dirt stuck to my navel?
Or between the sway of grass,
as fluid as I came,

in the middle of a storm,
rain rinsing blood,
or washed ashore with the foam,
as salty as I'll become?

In Memory of You

I knew you but only
enough to think of you
when I'm writing poetry
or seeing through a lense,
brush in hand,
sea green pants,
bare feet kissing grass,
flowers and paint stains
dancing on my dress.

And thinking of you
was like the sun
setting on my regrets.
I envied you
even in death.
But death won't do
and wishing to die
would be
the worst way to honor you.

You are the morning sunrise,
beam of light and drip of honey
in the darkest corners,
on the bitterest tongue.
You are a brush stroke,
a turquoise ring,
a June bug, a belly laugh
teaching me from the grave
to lay barefoot in the grass.

Learning to Love

I awoke in a dream to find
a mountain rising
up out of my eyes;
gold trickled down its valleys,
snow swathed its peaks.
The sun cast an autumnal glow
on everything. No flesh pressed
against mine, the spaces between
my fingers stayed empty.

What made my heart call out to yours
when it was the mountains and trees,
the flora sprouting between their roots
that melted my heart to honey in my dreams?
Growing up without grass beneath your back
and dirt on your feet
tricks you to think someone else's
skin, bones, blood, and tendons
were meant to fill gaps
in the hands, crooks of limbs,
under the arms, between the legs,
along the subtle curve in the lower back.

But my heart was made for me,
and I was made from the earth.
My toes were meant to dig into the dirt,
fingers to splay in the grass,
arms to wrap around trees
with curved limbs to cradle my back.
And maybe there's room in my chest
for another pair of lungs,
maybe my skin can stretch
to cover yours,
but my limbs are too broken to carry another;
my heart is still learning to love its own skin.

Vulnerable

As I lie on my back, vertebrae stacked
up against the earth, the soles of my feet
uproot from the dirt
to meet in an Earth-stained kiss.
I drop my knees
out to the sides,
thighs splayed,
hips wide as in birth, as in tides churning
under moons, as in flowers
in bloom, unfolding
under wet April suns: light-soaked,
dew-skinned,
vulnerable to pollinators & probing hands.
I am fighting the urge
not to fold up and in,
to rush through winter,
through spring
into autumn.
You are not alone, she says.
But I am,
and I am.

Root to Rise

I explored my mind and my heart
like navigating a forest floor.
Some paths wound through tangled brambles,
some lead to open meadows.
Sometimes there was no path at all—
I felt my way through the corridors of my heart
with my hands stretched out, grasping
onto anything—tree sap,
rose thorns, the jagged edge
of a rock—even if it hurt,
even if I bled,
even if it embedded itself between fingernail and flesh.

I let the wounds
and the forest debris glued to them
become a part of me
until I was the forest, snaking through the dirt
at the roots,
scraping sky,
bearing fruit,
tangling and untangling
leaf-strewn branches,
hollowing out at the core
to let in the living.

Birds build nests
in the crooks of my arms,
squirrels cling to my back
to keep me warm,
lightning bugs & butterflies
escape from my lungs,
owls keep guard of my wounds,
scanning the woods
with their binocular eyes
so I can stand with my heart
open,
chest lifted,
feet grounded,
palms reaching
up, up, up
from root to rise.

Own Two Feet

Would you walk this Earth with me, knowing that
my knees sometimes wobble and my feet
often stumble and the ground is not
always solid or flat or marked clearly on maps?

I never know when I should go it alone
or hand-and-hand,
and I'm afraid I haven't done enough
of the latter.

And I'm glad my legs aren't solid:
they've uprooted me from the Earth.
And I'm glad my feet misstep because they wander,
that geography has taught me to adapt.

But had I done it on my own, my legs by now
would be a bit stronger, the soles of my feet
calloused and coated in dirt, hands free
to cradle the heart I forced you to coddle.

But if I could walk with you as you and not with you as my crutch,
I would fumble and fall and veer off path,
drop to my knees and crawl in circles,
and I know you'd be right there with me, down in the dirt.
Oh, the possibilities of my own two feet.

Soft Shells

I wanted only
to know my own heart,
to peel back old petals—
dry & dead as onion skin
—& find budding flesh.

Only
I mistook another's heart for mine
& forgot to look inward.
For years I hung inverted
from the ceiling,
drained of blood & oil & water,

everything that kept me soft
& tender.

But with age I've learned even
the toughest skin sloughs off
with files, exfoliants, & volcanic rock.

With time, patience, self love,
even the hardest shells turn soft.

Yoga

I fumble through the branches, brambles, and leaf-hidden roots of my mind. Skin scratched, shins bruised, head spinning. One moment I'm clawing through thickets and crawling through dirt, the next I'm curled up in a tree hollow on a damp creek bank wishing to be simultaneously visible and unseen. Either way, I'm stuck or spiraling, regretting or reaching, overwhelmed or utterly empty.

Until one day I learn to breathe. To sit with myself and observe what's inside me. To be mindful, present, and aware. My breath levels out, my heart steadies, my mind calms.

I learn to move my body in rhythm with my breath. To breathe in light and love and let go of that which does not serve me. To open my heart and mind to growth and possibility.

My breath is a steady roar of crashing waves guiding me down a clear path. My limbs move with intention, my feet find their way.

And when I reach a fallen tree, a rushing river, a dead end, or other obstacle in my path, I fight the urge to panic or run or curl up into myself. I practice awareness. I breathe. I sit with myself and observe what's inside me. Breath levels, heart steadies, mind calms.

Body moves with breath to navigate the branches, brambles, and tree roots of the mind. To find footing on rocky inclines. To find balance on a river's slick stepping stones. And when I bat open my eyes, I'm in a clearing in the woods, on the vast expanse of an ocean's shore, in the very center of a sprawling meadow, surrounded by open sky above, Earth below, honey bees and wildflowers flying and swaying all around me.

This is what yoga has taught me:

Be mindful.
Be present.
Find balance.
Stay centered.

Shavasana

Lying there, legs to earth,
arms pinned open like moth wings,
the gaping cradle of shavasana,
I glimpsed, between Earth's fluttering blinks,
clouds sailing
across fresh sky
& knew
that the universe was for me
& for every body
beside me,
for the grass beneath,
trees above,
earthworms squirming—milky white
—among their roots.
My soul drifted
to that spotless corner of my mind,
accessed only by an alchemy
of calm, breath,
& moon-lit, feather-fragile,
moth-wing-pinned vulnerability.
Throat exposed,
heart gaping,
I felt the earth
press back.

How to Live By The Seasons

I dipped my feet
toes first
into the cool, wet grass,
then into the earth.

If I stood tall
and still,
I was a spring deer
birthed from the woods.

If I sank down to a squat,
I was a frog
or a stone Buddha,
tinged blue in the summer dusk.

And when September peeled back
the leaves' soft green shells,
I stayed stark still
at the beauty of it.
I watched October rain
paint the leaves goldfish orange,
pomegranate crimson,
chestnut brown,
& sun-tinged lemon.
The sun set the trees ablaze,
and I watched them
shed the damp weight
of summer from their limbs.

By the cusp of winter,
my feet had iced over
up to the ankles.
My body had disrobed.
I was a pale maple
in a sea of violet & grey,
the faintest drip of indigo
caressing my skin.
A wisp of pink-orange cloud,
or my own sunset-tinged hair,
curled through the pale sky
as if to cling tight

A Time for Winter

to autumn,
as if to grab
the weighty warmth of the sloughed off past,
avoid the sting of winter
altogether.

I didn't want to lose everything,
but everything eventually contracts.

Wild

You've got a gift for getting lost
in the woods,

but instead of pulling out
your heart,
following its thumps and flutters,

you curl up,
burrow into the earth

because to hear the heart
you have to rip muscle,
crack a rib,

and blood is sticky
and thick.

But that's just it:
bones mend, muscles tear
so they can grow.

Blood is honey,
thick with us.

In the dark,
at the forks,
when wind chills your bones

and sways the trees
to slash your skin,

let them crack and bleed,
let your heart ache.
Feel everything.

In breaking,
the heart finds its way.

Body & Mind

When bodies bend and hearts break
minds blossom   like flowers
breaking free of ice cages.
We get too comfortable
there, wrapped up in fleece
and fine-tuned routines.

       But the body isn't made
for stagnancy;
the mind is meant to expand.
And someday,   maybe,
I'll accept you without judgment,
and you will do the same.

       Someday
I'll look myself in the mirror—
in the eyes, down the curves,
across the arid heart space and the bays
between my bones,
over the violet-veined skin stretched canvas tight
around them
—and know love.

Lunar

I.
Inhale: Imagine your belly
filling up with light.

II.
The waxing moon grows
at night
like a fetus in its womb.
In twenty-eight days,
she will birth a shadow.

III.
The full moon pulls me out
from the uterus, shedding
the sticky dust of infertility.
Hurricanes rage
in the canals of my anatomy.

IV.
The woman in me
bites her tongue,
hides her shadows.
The wolf runs wild:
howling up at the moon,
digging into the dirt,
blood on her jaw,
mud in her fur.

V.
Moon is mother
to newly hatched youths
crawling clumsily
to the sea.
She cannot protect them;
she can only call them home.

VI.
Exhale: Imagine your lungs expelling
that which does not serve.
The abdomen swells
to a moon.

Let it feed the wolf to teach the woman
so both may run wild
naked through the trees,
barefoot on the earth.

On The Exhale

Some days I feel like I'm wading through mist.
I can't see what's ahead
or what's behind (probably for the best).

It gets heavier, doesn't it?
At least that's what I think on the days
I can't breathe.

I coax my lungs to dig deep:
in through the nose,
out through the mouth,

in the nose, out the mouth,
in, out,
in—

the mist lifts on an exhale
to reveal a quiet and limitless wood
with pathways blossoming in every direction.

Soul Work

To be brave.
To be bold.
To carry my head high
& my shoulder blades low
& pulled back.
To expand the chest,
that precious heart space.
To trust my gut.
To find my voice.
To speak from heart & soul.
To unfold.
To run wild.
To be patient & kind.
To nurture my inner child.
To feel at home in my own skin.
To glow,
shed light.
To grow branches & blossom.
To love every piece of myself
whole.

I am getting there.
I am doing the work.
I am honoring.
I am shedding.
I am burning.
I am quieting.
I am rooting down.
I am rising.
I am moving forward,
some days in leaps,
some days in inches.

The time to bloom
is on the horizon—
watch me
as I am about
to blossom.

ACKNOWLEDGMENTS

To Mia. For constantly inspiring me with your intelligence, big life goals, and Leslie Knope drive. For talking to the quiet girl on that Europe trip. For staying in touch afterward. For talking true crime and law with me even though I have no idea what I'm talking about. For reminding me to vote. For sending me voter guides. For keeping me updated on politics. SSDGM—we need you in Congress or the White House some day.

To Jessica. For reading all my sappy, angsty, love-sick poems in college. For being my first real reader. For dragging me out of my shell freshman year of college. For all the drinks, laughs, and mutually understood looks from across the room. For your friendship that defies time and distance. I Tarzan.

To Carlos. For your brain and your patience. For always believing in and encouraging me. For accepting me—motor mouth, anxiety, silly songwriting outbursts, and all. For sticking with me through the dark times. For making me laugh. For sharing your mango with me. For helping me bring my greatest dream to life. I love you.

ABOUT THE AUTHOR

A Time for Winter is Kait Quinn's debut poetry collection. She lives, reads, writes, runs, and romanticizes in Minneapolis, Minnesota with her partner and their regal cat Spart. To learn more about Kait and her writing, visit her website at kaitquinn.com and follow her on Instagram at @kaitquinnpoetry.

Made in the USA
Columbia, SC
14 January 2021